MADONNA AND CHILD
Terra Cotta Rondel by Giovanni della Robbia
National Museum, Florence, Italy

COLOR IN ARCHITECTURE

BY

F. S. LAURENCE

EXECUTIVE SECRETARY, NATIONAL TERRA COTTA SOCIETY

NATIONAL TERRA COTTA SOCIETY

NEW YORK

PRINTED IN THE UNITED STATES OF AMERICA

———

DESIGNED BY J. M. BOWLES   PRINTED BY SIDNEY A. STORER, NEW YORK

LIST OF ILLUSTRATIONS

❧

LIST OF ILLUSTRATIONS (*Continued*)

COLOR PLATES

FOREWORD

⁂

THE previous appearance in brochure form of some of the matter contained in this volume has led to many requests from members of the architectural profession for an amplified issue with the addition of further color plates. This revised and enlarged edition of "Color in Architecture" has been prepared with the hope that it may in some degree meet the desire so expressed. New color plates and black and white illustrations have been added, replacing some of those originally appearing.

Color illustrations include a number of purely imaginary buildings prepared only for their suggestive value in the application of color to such types. They do not presume to any instructive aim in the formal aspects of architectural design nor to prescribe any precise uses or methods of coloration. Complete elevations are included merely to symbolize types of buildings in which the use of color is particularly appropriate; also to enable the architect to visualize readily the relation of the detail studies to the types of building for which they have been conceived and the effect in ensemble of the use of color suggested. In some cases colored illustrations are given of buildings designed by architects and actually erected, renderings being from the architects' original studies and sketches made after erection.

The imaginary skyscraper subjects which reflect the requirements of the modern zoning law restrictions typify a form of construction to whose satisfying æsthetic interest color is coming to be recognized as an organic necessity. The logical nature of this newer type of skyscraper design manifests itself in the prevailing tendency to eliminate widely projecting cornices and other overhanging features and to replace these and the interest of shadow with an element which will more appropriately enhance the dominant interest of silhouette and mass in this type of building. For this purpose color presents itself inevitably as the most promising solution.

To the extent that any of the renderings of imaginary buildings of this or other type may be deemed worthy of adaptation for any contemplated project, their use in this way by architects will not be regarded as infringement of the copyright restrictions. The hope is, however, that these plates with the accompanying text will serve rather to stimulate the exercise of the architect's own ideas in the use of color; recognizing that while the employment of polychrome in architecture can never be wholly empirical nor pursued in disregard of the basic laws of coloration so well observed for instance in the great periods of Grecian, Gothic and Renaissance architecture, neither can the employment of color be reduced to a mere use of formulas uninspired by the promptings of personal feeling, taste and creative imagination. In the handling of color we deal with an art, not a definite and exact science.

This book is offered therefore with the modest hope that it may at least succeed in encouraging endeavor to attain satisfying solutions in the use of polychrome and assist the architect to achieve these in his own way. With the exception of the color plates appearing on pages 19 and 27 all color renderings and the designs of imaginary subjects are the work of Rudolph De Ghetto. The treatise on the basic principles encountered in chromatic problems originally appeared as a series of articles published in "The American Architect and Architectural Review" during the months of September and October, 1922, permission to republish having been courteously accorded by the editors of that magazine. With some revision of the text designed to give it more specific value for the designer's library it may be found to contribute in some small measure to the splendid results which await a confident employment of more color in our contemporary architecture.

COLOR IN
ARCHITECTURE

VERY building erected necessarily presents a color scheme. The following pages aim to give some of the broad fundamental principles of the successful use of color through employment of the materials which must be the medium of its expression in architecture. Literature that is of practical help in this relation is unfortunately quite limited. A number of works exist on the phenomena of color, the laws of harmony and theory of complementary shades, among which Chevreul's work, translations of which may be found in our public libraries, presents the most complete and exhaustive treatment of the subject. This and similar literature, however, is all so highly technical and scientific that there is need of a simple statement of the basic principles of application in architecture and the use of available mediums.

The first necessity is a correct interpretation of the term "color." In the employment of the word there is much confusion of thought, "color" being too frequently used to define only an expression in polychrome design and usually to denote the treatment of detail in shades of green, blue, yellow, etc. The term polychrome is also used sometimes to describe contrasts of tone in one color or in black and white, which may also be used to enrich ornament or define pattern.

Consideration of the subject should start with recognition of the term "color" as covering any possible result in the use of any material, whether in one or in several colors. There is no material employed in architecture which has not color, whether it be any of the varieties of natural stones, marble, brick, terra cotta or even cement. All have a certain chromatic interest proceeding from the nature of the elements composing them even where no artificial color interest is introduced in manufacturing or finishing processes. White and black, which are not colors in the strict meaning of the term, nevertheless have a positive interest which may be described as chromatic and for the purposes of this article will be included under the term color as hereafter used.

The statement that every building erected presents a color scheme is something more than the trite expression of an undisputed fact. It brings into view the law of association in mental process which must be taken into account in solving the color problems of architectural design.

INFLUENCE OF FAMILIAR EXAMPLES: SINCERITY

To realize the importance of this factor apply a test easily open to the resident of any average American city. Stroll through any of the streets and note the number of familiar buildings which have not heretofore registered on your consciousness an impression of any chromatic interest. You will be surprised to note the gamut of color represented in these familiar instances, taking the street as a whole. Here are a few colors noted in the space of one city block in the midtown business section of New York, referring only to materials used in construction and excluding awnings, signs, and other accessories: red, green, blue, yellow, brown, gray, purple, black and white, in quantity, and in great variety of each color.

To mention the effect, or non-effect, upon consciousness, of one very positive color by way of illustration. Red greets us on every hand in the façades of brick buildings and is dismissed

9

EDUCATION BUILDING, UNIVERSITY OF TEXAS, AUSTIN, TEXAS
Cass Gilbert, Architect

In this building polychrome terra cotta has been combined with brick and limestone in a carefully studied scheme including the use of blues, whites, yellows and touches of red throughout the frieze and ornamental panels between brackets, the spandrel features under third story windows and details of the sill course at the same level.

as not illustrating any use of color from its prevalence as a familiar commonplace. The attitude of mind would be markedly different were the same color, identically, to be used as a field for the walls of a stucco dwelling, or such a modification of it as would register on the eye an equal intensity of prevailing color to that occasioned by the brick and mortar joint together. Here we would have the impression of a "color stunt" and probably a quite ugly one at that. Now why? Cement can be artificially colored and given an interesting broken texture. Delicate pink, a modification of red, would not offend. This, and various shades of yellow and gray are beautiful and perfectly legitimate in stucco. Why not red, and as bright as obtainable in any brick? Red walls are beautiful when expressed in skillful brick design. Why not in stucco? There is nothing in the laws governing the harmonious relation of colors in the abstract and their application to structural form which forbids.

The answer is to be found in our habit of associating certain color effects with certain materials, and no effective study can proceed which ignores this as a powerful factor in solving the problems of chromatic treatment. But it does not follow that we are bound by it against any departure from the sphere of familiar things nor that doing so necessarily involves something more startling and bizarre than what we already have in "safe" conservative examples of design. Looked at with new eyes some of these are pretty pronounced chromatic "stunts" measured by the standards of abstract color relationships.

But the use of color in architecture cannot be reduced to the abstract and be determined by any pure theory of color and the principles of harmony alone. In architecture color cannot be disassociated from the problems of formal expression and the significance in this of the materials used. The nature of material should be evident. This is enforced by the principles of organic constructional design. The materials

DETAIL OF EDUCATION BUILDING, UNIVERSITY OF TEXAS, AUSTIN, TEXAS
Cass Gilbert, Architect
For use of color see caption to illustration of this building, page 10.

should retain and show the characteristics with which nature and necessary process endow them or admit applying to them fittingly, as in the case of paint upon wood. Manufactured products having definitely marked characteristics in color enforced by essential process, like brick, terra cotta and various ceramics, should hold to these qualities of coloring and those which the mind will instinctively recognize as appropriate to their nature. Without observance of this the first great principle of all vital design, sincerity, cannot be realized.

QUALITY AS AN ELEMENT OF COLOR

Granting the correct interpretation of the term color to mean the chromatic interest of an

PORTION OF FAÇADE, LIBRARY, UNIVERSITY OF TEXAS, AUSTIN, TEXAS
Cass Gilbert, Architect

The handsome polychrome effect in this building has been attained through the use of very richly painted decoration in the soffit of the wood cornice, the polychrome terra cotta frieze, rondels and architraves framing the large windows. Walls are buff limestone, polychrome ornament in the terra cotta and cornice involving the prevailing use of blues, yellow and white with minor touches of other coloring.

entire building, we are brought to the question of how far we can proceed to a consideration of the uses of color from the sound basis of sincerity defined in the preceding chapter as the first principle for observance. Before attempting any outline of the further principles of use to be observed, there remains the fundamental matter of appreciating the meaning of the term "quality" as applied to color, since without this no observance of the principles of harmony and contrast in the relationship of colors to one another enables a result satisfying to the cultivated æsthetic sense. As a rule professional readers need no definition of the term as generally used in art; those who may be less familiar with the use of color may identify "quality" as that characteristic in which unpleasant harshness and

crudity are not only avoided, but the effects produced are attended with a positive charm not readily described. Perhaps the word sympathy may express it. This quality may be found in colors of the strongest brilliance and carrying power as well as in tints of the subtlest delicacy. The term may also denote the qualification of one color toward the characteristics of another. Broadly, however, it refers to the characteristic which gives any color an appeal to the cultivated æsthetic sense.

Recognition of what constitutes "quality" in a single shade unrelated to other colors is the first essential to realizing it in a complex of many colors occurring in the terms of a design. Both in his scholastic training and subsequent practice the architect is obliged, however, to work

CHURCH OF THE MISSION SAN JOSÉ DE AGUAYO, SAN ANTONIO, TEXAS

Founded in 1720

Constructed entirely of stone, the walls were afterwards surfaced in stucco and brilliantly colored by the application of paint, traces of which still remain. These early missions were almost invariably executed in brilliant polychrome, usually in a form of sgraffito, the entire structures blazing with color from the ground level to topmost pinnacles of the towers. The superbly carved main portal of this building was executed in a soft variety of native stone of very pale buff shade.

RESTAURANT, 21ST STREET AND BOARDWALK, CONEY ISLAND, N. Y.
Dennison & Hirons, Architects

An adaptation of Spanish precedent liberally interpreted in the details of ornament and carried out in polychrome
terra cotta and stucco, the general color scheme being shown on the opposite page.

largely in black and white and this does not tend to his visualizing in terms of color. A course of landscape sketching in color pursued systematically through later practice, as many architects indeed do for recreation, would go far to equipping the designer with that sensitive appreciation of qualities, tones and values of color which would vivify his creations with the color quality they sometimes do not possess. Close study of the extreme subtleties of nature's color palette under varying conditions is the best training of the color sense yet afforded by any line of study, providing only that the follower of architecture continues to recognize the necessary self-assertion of the mediums of the latter art, considered as material, and does not allow his point of view in that relation to be swamped by the painter's disregard of it in realizing the effects of pictorial composition. An analogy to this exists in the respective problems of presentation encountered by the painter and the sculptor. One works from the standpoint of simulating form and the other from the standpoint of actually realizing it. The

architect, like the sculptor, must realize in tangible form and must preserve this expression against any tendency to obscure this in the application of color which the aims of the painter might entail.

FORM SHOULD REMAIN DOMINANT

This brings us to the second principle in an intelligent use of color in architecture—that form must remain dominant and coloration emphasize and sustain this dominance. Here an analogy may best be drawn from the problem of the mural painter in properly preserving the sense of wall surface and not making holes of his wall panels. The mural decorations of Puvis de Chavannes illustrate the complete observance of this principle in their masterly subordination to the requirements of surface and architectural form.

It is in this point that much of what has been written casually on the subject in relation to architecture proceeds eventually up a side track and halts dead against the bumper of an inflex-

WINDOW ORNAMENT IN POLYCHROME TERRA COTTA ON CORNER PIERS
OF RESTAURANT AT CONEY ISLAND, N. Y.

Dennison & Hirons, Architects

Color rendering sketched from the completed work after its erection. Prior to execution full
size plaster casts of all detail were made, painted to represent the color effects desired and tried out
in corresponding out-door positions.

TWO OF A SERIES OF RONDELS FOR THE EXTERIOR OF RESTAURANT AT CONEY ISLAND, N. Y.
Dennison & Hirons, Architects
Modeled by Max Keck and executed in polychrome glazes from cartoons and plaster models colored by Duncan Smith. The coloring is in blue, green, vermilion and gold glazes.

ible formula. We have it from several authorities that "color should not be employed upon supporting members as its use tends to obscure form and destroy the sense of supporting function." In any proper understanding of the term "color" how is its use to be avoided in these members? Color is everywhere with us in every material used and on the theory propounded a brick pier conveys no sense of support and the use by the late Stanford White of richly colored granite for the columns of the portico of the Madison Square Presbyterian Church in New York was a chromatic misapplication. Theories are useful when they are the servants and not masters of thought and action. All we can safely deduce in this relation is the general principle that the choice and application of colors must not tend to destroy the sense of support or of form where these should remain evident. Just what use of color will or will not do so in a given instance remains for the eye to determine by trial. It is easy to conceive that contrasting colors applied horizontally to a column would so break its vertical continuity of appearance as to destroy the sense of its mass and supporting function when a vertical use of the same colors might not do so. Also that the use of a single pronounced dark color for a detached column against a background of the same color might so lose the column to sight that the surmounting entablature would be left hanging in the air.

The first step should be a color sketch for the effect in ensemble of the whole building. This should precede final scale drawings and full-size details. Some architects find a colored cardboard model preferable. It is also best to have duplicate plaster casts made of certain full-size models of important detail and work out the color scheme to finality on these. This involves very little extra expense to the architect and is highly desirable, as color may have to be intensified in the full size to approximate the relational effects indicated in the small-scale model or drawing, delicate indications in the latter sufficing in its small scale but becoming anæmic if matched in full size. Coloring of full-size casts when employed can be with tempera or ordinary oil paints but in all such cases a series of colored terra cotta samples in the form of small tile blocks should be at hand for approximating the qualities of color obtainable under ceramic process. Where effect of full glaze instead of matt finish is desired this may be accomplished by varnishing afterward.

17

It also remains for the eye to determine by trial the effectiveness of color relations upon form as these may occur in frieze, pediment, cornice, architrave and all other elements of structural design. Similarly the theory of complementary colors and their mutually enhancing effect is a resource to be employed within the broad reservation that what constitutes taste and will yield that jealously cherished objective, "safety" of design in its visual aspect, is something that no rule can assure.

There can be no progress, however, if timidity is to rule in this regard. With the wealth of successful precedent existing in the lavish use of polychromy by the ancient Greeks, the rich resources for inspiration also to be found in the terra cotta architecture of Renaissance Italy, not to mention the ceramics of Moresque Spain and the superb instances of oriental tile work in Persia, it is difficult to see why a more confident and widespread employment of color has not been attempted in contemporary architecture. The materials exist in the resources of modern manufacture in very much broader degree, and public acceptance of the result is merely a matter of its familiar presence.

UNITY OF CHROMATIC ENSEMBLE

Unity is another fundamental principle in

"ASSUMPTION OF THE VIRGIN" ALTAR PIECE IN ENAMELED TERRA COTTA BY ANDREA DELLA ROBBIA, METROPOLITAN MUSEUM OF ART, NEW YORK CITY

An example of Andrea's work now in America. The heads of the Virgin, one cherub and three of the standing figures are modern restorations. These restorations suggest the ready possibility of approximating the splendid effects of original Robbia sculpture in modern terra cotta. The coloring of this example is the characteristic use of white figures on a blue ground with touches of other color in the minor details.

successful color design. Such an application of color as would tend to destroy the appearance of structural function would, of course, violate the requirements of formal design, however the use of color might hold together as mere chromatic composition. Considered in the latter relation purely, unity may be assured either by the proportional dominance of some one shade to which all others are consistently keyed in subordination or the result may be obtained by a distribution of two or more colors that combine in a textural presentation as one color of some generally prevailing cast. Of this latter character are the turquoise appearing domes of certain Persian mosques which are really in polychrome tile of intricate pattern. In polychrome schemes this principle of coloring for the field masses carries better assurance of unity than a preponderant mass of perfectly plain color broken only at wide intervals by units of design in other colors which recall themselves by repetition. Here there is introduced the chance that too wide separation or the differing qualities of various materials may not hang well together, and will tend to dissect the design. A design embodying the use of terra cotta panels in marble, stone or brick walls will hold together perfectly if well done while uses of trim differing markedly from wall surfaces both in color and texture are,

18

DETAIL OF PRIVATE HOUSE AT BRESCIA, ITALY

From "The Terra Cotta Architecture of North Italy"

Architect Unknown

Evidently one of the finest examples of painted polychrome decoration in cement and
terra cotta. This fragment is no longer available for first-hand study. Note the charm-
ingly harmonious shades of warm gray and the beautiful suggestion
for modern ceramic treatment in low relief.

MAJESTIC THEATRE, HOUSTON, TEXAS
John Eberson, Architect

An exceptionally successful polychrome result in which delicate shades of pastel coloring have been carried through
the terra cotta detail and softly mottled glazing of the ashlar, tying the whole into agreeable unity.

of course, customary and achieve the same result. In fact, such differences may be necessary to avoid monotony and properly express structural design but in general it will be found true that in polychrome schemes unity is best realized by carrying the colors used in polychrome ornament throughout the field also in some degree or manner duly subordinating their appearance there to the prevailing mass shade and to the focal points in their use occurring in the features of polychrome ornament. Sometimes this may transpire in the normal variations of the mass of field color occurring in the shade of each unit, as with certain kinds of brick, natural stones, marble and terra cotta, which recall corresponding shades in the ornamental features occasioned by shadow. Again, as with terra cotta, when this is used for ashlar as well as ornamental detail, it may be had through many of the varieties of mottled finish obtainable in terra cotta whereby the colors, or some one prevailing tint among

them, may be carried through the field in this way. As a treatment such mottling partakes of the character of the brush work employed in the school of painting popularly known as "impressionistic" and exemplified in the paintings of Claude Monet and the American Painter Childe Hassam.

Much the same distributive effect occurs in the black and white mottlings of various stones, granite particularly, and it is doubtless this consideration which to some degree dictates the tendency of many architects to demand imitations of granite in terra cotta. Color mottlings more distinctively ceramic can be had, however, in terra cotta and admit a richer interest than that of black and white or their blending into sombre gray effect.

Obviously it will be recognized that mere physical distribution of color alone in this or any repetitive way will not hold a chromatic result together if the colors employed are out of key with each other. The relationship of individual color notes and masses of color to each other in what may be called the octaves of composition has to be considered and nothing struck out of key.

HARMONY AND RICHNESS

With unity assured, the fullest chromatic richness becomes possible without offense to the eye or the most conservative æsthetic taste. What offends is not brilliance and richness of coloring. It is harshness and lack of harmony. An oriental rug may carry the splendors of an Arabian treasure chest in amethyst, ruby and sapphire coloring yet take its place perfectly without clash in any soberly quiet interior. So may the front of a building in the grayest of conservative city streets.

Harmony as a basic requirement is necessarily bound up with any unity of effect and in the use of pure and unqualified colors is a matter of well defined law. As the finest relations in this respect occur in the joint use of intermediate and qualified shades, no set rules can be formulated as to colors which will and will not harmonize when placed together. Harmony is a complex result and proportionate use for one thing plays a great part in it. Beyond saying that colors must exhibit consistent "quality" it is impossible to say what will and will not harmonize among them. I know of no two colors which cannot be so qualified in character that, while still justifying their original designations, they cannot be made to harmonize, even such unlikely combinations as brown and pink.

In general it is well, however, for users of color to proceed conservatively in the employment of a few simple shades of familiar harmonious quality until mastery of more complex relations has been obtained through eye practice, but we should dismiss at once that form of timidity which reduces the positiveness of coloring to washed-out versions of colors in the hope that their weakness will avoid offense and give a "safe" result. The most anæmic version of any color in the palette may exhibit a harsh and unpleasing quality. In water color, for instance, a raw harsh blue will remain a raw harsh blue, dilute it with water as we may.

In this connection, atmosphere and sunlight are often good friends to a composition reflecting these characteristics. The carrying power of certain colors as appearing in samples of material at close hand will often be found to vary widely under these influences, tending in the main toward reduction of intensity, as in the case of blues at a height and the mellowing and pulling of all together into agreeable harmony.

APPLICATION OF COLOR TO ORNAMENT

In general it will be found that polychromatic treatment of ornament admits, and in most

DETAIL OF POLYCHROME TERRA COTTA ORNAMENT IN FAÇADE
OF MAJESTIC THEATRE, HOUSTON, TEXAS
John Eberson, Architect

22

HERALDIC DETAIL IN POLYCHROME TERRA COTTA UPON FLANKING TOWERS
OF THE UNION RAILROAD STATION, HAVANA, CUBA

Kenneth M. Murchison, Architect

Executed in gold and matt glazes.

MADISON SQUARE PRESBYTERIAN CHURCH, NEW YORK CITY

McKim, Mead & White, Architects

An epochal modern achievement in the successful relation of brick, granite, marble and terra cotta. The completion of this work greatly stimulated interest in the possibilities of polychrome design in America and may be regarded as initiating the present widespread production of polychrome glazes in exterior terra cotta. Destruction of this building to make way for a skyscraper has been justly regarded as a distinct loss to American architecture. The tympanum feature of the pediment has been preserved by permanently installing in one of the wings of the Metropolitan Museum of Art, New York City

MOOLAH TEMPLE, ST. LOUIS, MO.
Helfensteller, Hirsch and Watson, Architects
Moresque precedent adapted in brick and terra cotta brilliantly enriched with polychrome glazes
in the ornamental detail.

cases, makes preferable, a lower relief modeling than would be advisable for the same form if executed in monochrome. In the latter, shadow must be relied upon to define pattern to greater or less degree. With a colored background relief ornament is thrown into definition by color contrast mainly. The presence of too much shadow blending with the usually darker color of the background tends to soften and in some cases obliterate definiteness of pattern. It may also tend to obliterate form. Modeling therefore should proceed with the view to the use of color contemplated, especially in a polychrome feature. This may involve the question also of separating adjoining shades of strong contrasting colors with a fillet, carrying the ground color between them after the manner frequently pursued in polychrome ornament by the ancient Greeks; or in ceramic mediums, by raised edge terminations to certain spaces sufficient to arrest the flow of glaze in firing without showing actual separation to the eye.

Various refinements may be employed to give or emphasize the significance of retreating and advancing surfaces. It is a well-known axiom of the painters' studio that "indoors, lights are cool and shadows warm; outdoors, lights warm and shadows cool." The application to problems of exterior and interior color treatment in architecture is evident. Similarly, adjoining masses of color may be made to assume greater or less degrees of warmth by contrast of qualities in this regard. They may even be given an appearance of a different cast of coloring, a vivid spot of red, for instance, which is the complement of green, intensifying the latter or imparting a greenish cast to an adjoining gray.

Available Mediums

In considering the various mediums which may be used to express color in the form of polychromatic design, clay products are the most prolific in yielding resources for the most varied treatment. Under this heading we have many beautiful shades of brick carrying a number of interesting surface textures, ceramic tile in a multiplicity of glazes and decorative designs, several shades in glazed and unglazed roofing

WINDOWS IN THE COURT OF THE PALACE OF GALEAZZO VISCONTI
AT PAVIA, NEAR MILAN, ITALY

From "The Terra Cotta Architecture of North Italy"

From a restoration made in 1867 by F. Lose. Bernardino of Venice appears to have been among the architects responsible. This once magnificent 14th Century dwelling shows today no evidence of its original polychrome splendor, some of the terra cotta detail together with the marble originally used for the spandrels and wall surfaces between the brick piers and windows having been stripped off and no vestige now remaining of the painted decoration.

UPPER STORIES, MATSON BUILDING, SAN FRANCISCO, CALIFORNIA
Bliss & Faville, Architects

Typical of the restrained use of polychrome which has heretofore characterized its employment in skyscraper design.
General color of terra cotta warm gray throughout with background of ornamental features in blue green.

tile and faience and architectural terra cotta in a great variety of surface finishes, textures and colors, both glazed and unglazed. All may be used together and in conjunction with certain stones and highly colored marbles in effects of the most sumptuous richness. Excepting in terra cotta the use of any one medium alone for complete color effect carries a chance of inorganic formal expression as there are features in design and ornament not possible to realize in brick nor in tile owing to the small and uniform character of their unit construction and consequent scheme of jointing. In tile the color range is very wide but its essential character as a veneer forbids its use to organically express construction in ornamental forms frequently employed for that purpose or having such implication. Terra cotta is not subject to this limitation, as it may take the form of veneer or be produced in the special

shapes, sizes and modeled relief essential for organic constructional expression. Diaper patterns, for instance, in terra cotta pieces of about twelve inches or greater dimension may be employed for the field of wall surfaces giving a tile veneer effect and can be combined with terra cotta column, cap, architrave, pilaster, cornice, bracket, and sculptural ornamentation in the great variety of form in which these elements occur in various styles. Owing to this flexibility for formal expression the use of terra cotta for practically the entire finish of a façade becomes possible without carrying the feeling of a too wholesale use of one material or a use which does violence to its nature in certain parts of the design.

THE INTEREST OF COLOR VARIATION

In considering the uses admitted by the very

29

DETAIL OF ENTABLATURE, WILMINGTON PUBLIC LIBRARY, WILMINGTON, DELAWARE

E. L. Tilton and A. M. Githens, Architects

Among the more recent adaptations of classic precedent in the use of color this building attains a very high degree of success in its chromatic aspect through a well conceived treatment in the terra cotta frieze which employs deep yellow, buff, gray and blue for the coloring, harmonizing with the limestone employed for the structural members below and plain wall surfaces of the façade. This joint use of stone and terra cotta presents interesting possibilities, each material in its qualities of color and texture serving as an admirable foil for the other.

wide range of colors and textures obtainable in terra cotta the natural tendency of all ceramic products to exhibit a certain variation of shade occurring in the process of firing should be recognized as one of the greatest sources of charm available for interesting chromatic effect. The history of brick manufacture illustrates the enormous progression in taste from the era of the uniform, smoothly finished, red pressed brick with its immaculately painted white stripe joint, so lavishly employed in the early seventies, to the pronounced variation of shade, texture and uneven form of the most deservedly popular varieties in use today. In roofing slate we have also gotten away from the smooth, uniform color and size once demanded in this product, and recognize the overpowering charm of the irregu-

larly mottled weathering slate with broken edges in differing thicknesses and sizes which our quarries are now yielding to the great enhancement of our country house architecture.

Similarly in terra cotta and other lines of ceramic material it is to be hoped that the slight eccentricities of fire will be allowed to assert themselves more freely and that the present standard of taste in using terra cotta, which reflects too much the attitude toward brick in the early seventies, will yield to an appreciation of the finer possibilities obtained through exploiting the natural variations of color and slight inaccuracies of form incident to ceramic manufacture rather than wishing to suppress them. When architects at large will express their conceptions in terra cotta with the crisp freedom of

SUGGESTION FOR COLOR TREATMENT OF A SKYSCRAPER
This imaginary motif contemplates in the main an all terra cotta treatment.

a loosely handled water color in wash we may look for results of incalculable significance and beauty in the architecture of our time.

This applies not only to effects in polychrome design but to schemes in which the color interest is that of simple monochrome treatment. In the first chapter it was pointed out that the proper application of the term "color" covers the chromatic result of the entire building and not simply those details which are executed in polychrome. As no building erected fails to present an aspect of color it suggests a word upon the element of form in ornamentation as contributing to this color aspect in the characteristic of shadow which must necessarily modify the tonal effect.

The choice of material determines in large measure the value and influence of shadow color in the chromatic ensemble. The varieties of soft stone commonly used in Spain for many of the most interesting and rich examples of Spanish renaissance were of a color that, under the brilliant sunlight of the Spanish climate, glowed with an appealing warmth casting shadows of a deep golden sienna that are in themselves positive color notes of the most charming quality. Naturally such profuse opulent richness of ornament in such a medium provides an interest both of form and color which does not need the further enrichment of applied polychrome coloring to realize a quite sumptuous chromatic quality. That this latter, however, occurs largely through the warmth of actual coloring of the stone itself is apparent in the fact that the golden quality of shadow is occasioned largely by reflected warm light from the parts illuminated by sunshine. A corresponding elaboration of carved treatment in a cold, gray variety of

TERRA COTTA DETAIL, PALAZZO FAVA, BOLOGNA, ITALY

An early Italian example in unglazed red terra cotta. See similar modern application illustrated on page 34.

material would occasion a shadow lacking in this positive effect of glowing color, being apt to take on a cooler cast of gray emphasizing the absence rather than the presence of color. Thus the nature of material must to some degree govern the result in counting upon the effect of shadow as an element of chromatic interest.

It is apart from the purpose of this treatise to discuss the weathering of materials as an element of color interest. Its charms in the varieties of products susceptible to it are altogether too well known to need description and they are moreover something which are not within the power of the architect to manipulate. They can be counted upon with fair certainty but must await the touch of the subsequent collaborator, Time. They cannot, therefore, be brought under the principles governing the preparation of design in polychrome as commonly understood. But it would be misleading to infer that the possibilities of color interest rest entirely in the use of polychrome composition. While true that there is no material which does not present the aspect of color of some description it is unfortunately the case that in this country under the conditions of local atmosphere in the greater part of it, the materials which are commonly available for monochrome effects do not carry the qualities which produce the luminous shadow that can count as a distinct color note. Here again the great variety of warm tints obtainable in our clay products yields a possibility analogous to that carried by the soft mellow stones and marbles of Italy and Spain, many of the ivory and light buff shades in terra cotta and brick holding a wealth of shadow color of the most sumptuous richness.

33

INTIMATE APPLICATIONS

The foregoing chapters have dealt entirely with the subject of exterior color in architecture. The chromatic treatment of interior design is a subject in itself which does not fall under the use of color as contemplated in this treatise. Nevertheless, materials which are used for exterior finish are so often applied to the permanent architectural features of interior spaces that a few words may well be added upon certain aspects of design in this field.

The merits of our various native stones and American and European marbles, particularly the richer colored varieties of these, are altogether too well known to require more than passing mention as familiar resources for chromatic effects in such applications. To some degree this is true also of the better lines of cement and other composition finishes widely employed in various appropriate ways. Knowledge of technique in all these familiar mediums requires but little, if any, amplification. But in the employment of ceramics as a medium for color expression there is a field of fresher interest which may be profitably explored in certain essentials not always realized in the use of this class of materials.

In common with the attitude which has largely characterized the employment of terra cotta for exterior use, the demand is too often to express the interest of marble or stone effects in form, color and surface texture, rather than striking directly for the equally high quality

DETAIL OF TERRA COTTA COLUMNS AND ARCH MOULDS, PERSHING SQUARE BUILDING, NEW YORK CITY

York & Sawyer and John Sloan, Architects

Reflecting the similar early Italian use illustrated on page 33 but executed in fire flashed terra cotta in shades varying from buff to golden brown.

which a ceramic medium is capable of giving in its own way. The broad principles enunciated for the use of material in exterior design apply equally to interior work, some of them assuming very acute importance under the intimacy of application and proximity to the eye. This fact is generally well appreciated and it is perhaps due to the influence of more familiar habit in employing color for interior uses in other mediums that the handling of it in ceramics for interior applications has been attended with a little more freedom and confident decision. In fact, certain freer uses of tile work have inclined too much toward the wholesale employment of ceramic finish for entire interiors, floors, walls and ceilings, to the exclusion of the richer interest that might have been obtained by a judicious association of ceramic finish with the contrasting and supplemental qualities of other mediums. The beauty of ceramic modeling in its softness of contour and the free flowing plasticity of design which should accompany it nowhere receive a more effective foil than when intelligently related to the chaste purity of line, edge and surface finish which is the consistent attribute of marble. The latter used as a bordering feature often enriches the opposite charm of free plasticity in the ornamentation of a tile field. Again the relation may be equally fine when reversed, the ceramic material being used as a border in highly rich ornamental relief and the enclosed space kept severely plain. Decorative sense in the designer must determine the

SUGGESTION FOR COLOR TREATMENT OF A STORE BUILDING DEVOTED
TO THE SALE OF AUTOMOBILES

An imaginary motif contemplating the use of matt-glazed terra cotta.

extent or even fact in this relationship rather than any fixed rule or theory. A scheme of design may well call for the textural interest of ceramic surface and jointing as an element to be carried throughout the entire wall or floor space in an all-ceramic treatment, but in general it will be found that the eye seeks relief at some point through the differing qualities of a different medium and it is in this respect that the early European uses of material are so highly satisfying. The significant thing to be noted is that in instances where ceramics were employed they appear to have enjoyed the highest measure of appreciation as a fitting vehicle for the most elegant effects in palatial treatment and that we do not find the gaucherie of view which regards only the most costly mediums as appropriate for such results. It is quite clear that della Robbia worked in glazed clay from preference and that many of the applications of his brilliant genius were designed in his favorite medium of ordinary clay—common inexpensive earth coated with colored enamels. The fact is significant when viewing the resources of his time in the liberal patronage of princely houses amply

STORE FRONT IN POLYCHROME TERRA COTTA,
STUTZ MOTOR CAR COMPANY,
CHICAGO, ILL.

Michaelson and Rognstad, Architects.

A light mottled gray was used for the ground color of the terra cotta, employing a deeper mottled gray for the main features of relief, with minor detail picked out in white, yellow, dark brown and black. Roofing tile, green glaze.

able to pay for use of the most expensive mediums for sculptural and decorative effect.

That this attitude did not apply merely to individual works of art in which the concept of the sculptor or painter was everything and the medium used of minor consequence is evident from the many applications of della Robbian faience to purely architectural uses in the finish of ceilings like that of the Chapel of the Madonna in the Impruneta and various tabernacles, ornamental friezes, etc. While these instances were usually of minor extent this was due clearly to the fact that the knowledge of how to apply colored enamels to architectural forms rested wholly with a family group of individual craftsmen not enjoying the facilities for extensive production in this direction. Otherwise we may be sure that the wonderful resources of their art would have been used to beautify extensively both the interiors and exteriors of many of the noblest structures of the time. This is borne out by the fact that contemporary Italian architecture of the period exhibited a widespread use of terra cotta lavishly colored with impermanent pigments which naturally

SACRED HEART CHURCH, NEW ORLEANS, LOUISIANA
Emile Weil, Architect.   Albert Bendernagle, Associate Architect
Unglazed polychrome terra cotta detail in relation with brick. Colors used:
yellow buff, light blue, delicate green and red.

would not have been employed if permanent glazes had been commonly available.

PRECEDENT AND INITIATIVE

The della Robbia family and their immediate successors did not know how to produce a matt surface glaze, much less one having any textural interest. This circumstance suggests another aspect in the resources of modern ceramics for appropriate finish which are open to the architect today. All the examples of the della Robbian school are in smooth bright enamels having a glassy sheen which tends to obscure form by its reflecting action, particularly in its susceptibility to glittering high lights. The original enamels of Luca della Robbia were somewhat softer in this respect than those of his successors but still embodied this drawback to the most satisfying expression. Had Luca known how to saturate his glaze compounds with elements producing a minute crystallization of the surface which eliminates the glitter he would certainly have turned to this resource with the most unbounded enthusiasm. It is in this development that modern ceramics present a medium surpassing that employed by della Robbia. In modern terra cotta and tile matt as well as bright glazes are freely obtainable and in surface textures of the greatest charm. Added to this are the very much greater range and variety of colors which the modern ceramic chemist has developed. With this increased facility for harmonious expression the matter of equal or superior results reduces itself to the quality of the architect's design and sculptor's modeling and is not a matter of rediscovering the secret of "a lost art" or of a medium of comparable excellence.

SUGGESTION FOR COLOR TREATMENT OF A SKYSCRAPER CONFORMING IN
DESIGN TO THE REQUIREMENTS OF RECENT
MUNICIPAL ZONING LAWS

An imaginary motif contemplating the joint use of polychrome terra cotta and brick.

TERRA COTTA CORNICE OF SMALL CHAPEL AT SIDE OF CATHEDRAL AT PARMA, ITALY

This ancient example was in unglazed red terra cotta and is a motif splendidly adapted to the constructional requirements of the modern zoning law skyscraper and to the use of polychrome treatment.

The very much greater range of possibility in ceramics now offered the designer suggests another point very vital to the appropriate and significant use of color in modern applications and one that applies whether the material be ceramics or any medium that may be employed for polychrome design.

Allusion has been made to the ample precedent which exists in the practice not only of the early Italians but of the ancient Greeks. It is natural that in any use of the classical orders, particularly the pure Greek, we should turn to the bright colors and shades of colors employed by the Greeks and apply them in the same way. Any use of the corresponding black, dull and bright reds, blues, brilliant yellow, gold and pure white should hold with certainty to the

method of distribution which modern research has established as characteristic of polychrome expression in Greek architecture. In fact, it is reasonably certain that the use of coloring was so studied and brought to such a state of final perfection in its technique that no departure in the use of corresponding colors could safely be made. But there is this very significant and vital factor to be remembered: such perfection of color technique must have rested inevitably upon the precise shades in coloring which the chemical knowledge of the ancient Greeks admitted producing. A virile strong race naturally found satisfaction in the use of positive strong colors and if not indisposed was at any rate unable to develop in the necessary mediums the wide gamut of subtle intermediate variations of color obtainable under the resources of more advanced chemical knowledge. Greek vase painting, for instance, exhibits none of the chromatic variety of ancient Chinese porcelains or Persian tile work nor do we find that the art of glazing their terra cotta extended beyond a process and result that more properly resembles burnishing. It is an interesting question what the Greeks would have done had they possessed facilities for the production of ceramic glazes in the wide range of various colors and intermediate shades of colors that exist today. Is it not probable that a race of such wonderful æsthetic sensibility would have quickly seized upon such resources, and if their use of colors in relation to form was influenced, as it must have been, by the characteristics of those colors, would they not necessarily have employed the differing colors and shades of a very much wider palette in a different way? One can scarcely conceive that they would not have used them at all and that the only shades they would have employed were precisely and identically the ones they did. They would have used electric light and changed their fixtures quickly enough if they had known how; and in the use of color who shall say that the road is not open

THE CHALIF STUDIOS, NEW YORK CITY
G. A. & H. Boehm, Architects

This building is an example of a very successful polychrome treatment. The base is South Dover marble of an ivory shade, the walls above being manganese brick in warm gray with architraves, paneling and frieze of polychrome terra cotta treated in ivory, golden yellow, soft sienna red and light green. Relief in the main is very flat. The whole ensemble is in beautiful harmony illustrating admirable restraint and an appreciation of subtle values.

to the modern architect to associate successfully the differing colors admitted by a modern palette with Greek or other classical ornament in a manner which the ancient Greeks would have accepted as perfectly satisfying? The possibility, of course, rests in an imagination gifted enough to do it successfully within the immutable principles which govern form in Greek art.

Correspondingly a slavish adherence to Persian, Arabic, or early Italian precedent in the use of color is nowhere enjoined by the facts of history or dictates of sound taste, admitting that in a repetition of any of these motives in design the law of association in mental process calls for a substantial adherence to the familiar chromatic aspects of such design for satisfying the mind in its sense of consistency. Beyond that there is no necessary bar to initiative.

A suitable palette of colors for application to architectural form is therefore not limited to any chromatic scale dictated by precedent. It preferably should include those tints and shades which have been employed in the best architecture of the past, but may confidently include varieties and interests of texture not among those known or available in former periods.

SUGGESTION FOR COLOR TREATMENT OF CORNICE IN THE UPPER
FEATURES OF A MODERN SKYSCRAPER
OF SET-BACK CONSTRUCTION

Materials brick and terra cotta. Comparatively low relief treated in this general
manner will carry effectivley at great heights, eliminating the necessity
of heavier projections.

TOMB OF CORTESIA SEREGA, CHURCH OF
SANT' ANASTASIA, VERONA

This rare and little known example of early Italian terra cotta was treated in
polychrome by painting the unglazed surface after firing, glazes having not
yet come into general use.

Modern ceramics already offer these in an as-tonishing range of very beautiful effects. In fact, the interest of technique occasionally suffers through a control which eliminates much of the charm arising from the more primitive processes employed in early European and Oriental ceramics. On the other hand, the compensating advantage of much broader chromatic scope and extent of application together with the facilities for obtaining material with the requisite speed for modern building operations could hardly be foregone for the satisfactions of more primitive charm. It is only in certain rare effects of luster in Hispano-Moresque and early Italian maiolicas and the superb porcelain glazes of ancient China that the modern ceramist has yet failed to excel technically in his production of material suitable for architectural application. The range of colors obtainable, for instance, in architectural terra cotta is given in the appendix and need not be elaborated here beyond saying that the laboratory formulas of the modern American manufacturer contain an infinite variety of each one of the colors enumerated in the appendix, in consistent gradations of these which can be supplied commercially and that the range is constantly expanding under further experiment. There is no need for the designer to depart from

45

EXAMPLES OF MODELING IN UNGLAZED BUFF TERRA COTTA WHICH EXPRESS WELL
THE QUALITY AND FEELING OF CLAY WORK
Warren & Wetmore, Architects

the obtainable varieties for any effect consistent with the nature of a ceramic medium, the problem in its practical commercial aspect consisting rather in the designer's appreciation of the fact that sumptuous richness can be achieved with a comparatively simple range of colors and a consistent employment of the warm and cool varieties of each color. But the attempt should not be made to express these in a working design without reference to ceramic samples illustrating the qualities of coloring resulting from the nature of ceramic process. These, it should also be remembered, occur from the action of chemical compounds subjected to a terrific heat for their development and this precludes a microscopic uniformity of shade among the units produced in any one prescribed color. Certain composite colors should also not be expected from the compounding of other colors which would yield these in the mixture of ordinary pigments. Distributive applications of one color over another or blending into another with this view, should therefore not be attempted in design without prior consultation with the manufacturer.

Both in tile and terra cotta as well as in the special developments in the latter which are properly known as faience, the color palette offered the architect today is ample for all purposes whose attainment can be reasonably de-

sired. No difficulty exists in this direction where the desire is not to torture out effects of coloring that belong properly to other mediums. It is not reasonable to hand a manufacturer of ceramics a piece of silk and say "match this" or to expect the same duplication from a piece of wall paper, wood, stone, marble or other substance when the material to be used is clay and when almost no color presented by any other substance fails to find a corresponding equivalent as color in the ceramic medium associated with a distinctive quality peculiar to the ceramic medium and constituting its essential dignity. The fact that the producers of ceramics have succeeded in many instances in successfully matching the characteristics of other materials under an enforced demand for this result in nowise changes the fact that the sincere designer will always prefer to use a material frankly for what it is and has ample resources for satisfaction in the profuse variety of effects which modern ceramic production now affords.

A word may be added in this connection respecting the exceedingly interesting possibilities offered by ceramics for pictorial mural decoration. Aside from the beautiful results in mosaic which are commonly familiar the possibilities of this in tile treatment are not as well understood as they might be. Demand in this direction has

ANOTHER SUGGESTION FOR COLOR TREATMENT IN TERRA COTTA FOR THE UPPER
PART OF A MODERN SKYSCRAPER

WETZEL BUILDING, NEW YORK CITY
Hill & Stout, Architects

This well-known example embodies detail treatment well repaying study. Polychrome interest has been closely associated with that of very rich textural charm in the brick and plastic hand made freedom of unglazed terra cotta ornament. Varying shades of soft golden brown in these materials are further set off by richly colored polychrome accents in glazed tile. This tile also exhibits the free, hand made quality of early ceramics in its irregular form and varying color.

exhibited on the whole a somewhat curious lack of appreciation of the immense dignity of effect obtainable. A whole chapter might well be written on this subject which pertains rather to that of interior decoration than the architectural use of color in a broad sense.

APPROPRIATE TECHNIQUE

UPPLEMENTING the foregoing chapters, a word should be added upon certain aspects of technique in the use of the clay products which today offer the principal opportunity for color expression.

Clay becomes usable for building purposes only after it has passed through a firing process reducing it to the necessary hardness. In this process all perishable substance in the clay is consumed and as the latter is a natural product, however refined by preparatory treatment, irregularities of form are bound to occur in the shrinkage resulting from this consumption. From what has been already said about variations of color similarly occurring, this corresponding formal limitation should be frankly accepted as belonging to the very nature of things in a ceramic product. Consistency in the use of such a medium requires that its nature in all points should be regarded, and coloring which is frankly ceramic demands form which is frankly ceramic. Similarly the quality of modeling in ornamental design should be that naturally yielded by the nature of wet clay before being dried and burnt. Wet clay cannot be chiseled and given the sharp edges of a finely grained marble or stone. The rigid character which is inseparable from the carving of a hard resisting substance has no place in the modeling of one which yields with the most plastic freedom to the touch of the bare

DETAIL FROM AN ANCIENT ITALIAN VILLA

Illustrating free treatment of terra cotta in line, form and finish, these qualities occurring naturally in the manufacture. Color is red, unglazed.

hand. Yet we find everywhere a demand that modeling in a product like terra cotta shall be finished "sharp and true," the result being that it often presents an aspect of mechanical rigidity entirely antithetic to the feeling of a yielding clay reduced to intense hardness by the freely playing action of flame.

The same applies to the results commonly demanded in jointing and alignment. An examination of the terra cotta work of the early Italians shows that they took their material as the kilns gave it to them, neither worrying about the frank presence of the necessary jointing nor seeking to reduce this to mechanical accuracy through grinding or other arbitrary treatment of the fired pieces. The result was that while their alignments and curves were to some extent broken and irregular, the effect, when associated with a consistently free treatment of modeling, exhibits all the charm of a freely handled crayon drawing, and it is this spirit which is appropriate to design in a clay material both in the treatment of form and the handling of color. On a previous page reference was made to the feeling of a loosely handled water color in wash and this we do not commonly associate in rendering with the tight precision of nicely finished pen drawing for the expression of line and form, much less any embodying use of the ruler and compass in the final touch. Clay mediums, in other words, present a possibility of realizing

SUGGESTION FOR THE ADAPTATION OF SPANISH PRECEDENT IN STUCCO AND TERRA COTTA
FOR A SMALL PUBLIC LIBRARY BUILDING

in actual construction the charm of free hand feeling which is often the compelling interest in a rendering—one that not uncommonly captures the imagination of the client (and sometimes a jury). We all know what a highly artistic drawing may convey in comparison with the coldly realized actuality of its execution in a building it is aimed to portray.

In this connection, some of our most accomplished architects have gone to extreme pains to secure in executed work results reflecting all the charm of early primitive process in various applications of tile and terra cotta. The difficulty that has been met in this respect has lain chiefly in the fact that technical improvement in all lines of ceramic production has resulted in bringing these mediums to the point where uncertainty in what will result under fire action has been largely eliminated. In chemical structure and the compounding of materials a similar certainty of command has likewise been achieved. In the manufacture of terra cotta, for instance, it has been found that by grinding and adding to the raw unfired clay a certain proportion of fired clay the unequal shrinkage formerly encountered in firing is largely overcome and the ware can be given a truer form and more even size than were formerly obtainable. Larger pieces can also be made, and in other respects a corresponding technical improvement of the highest practical value has been reached, greatly increasing the scope of possible applications. In all ceramic materials

ENTRANCE IN POLYCHROME TERRA COTTA, CHILDREN'S HOSPITAL, SAN FRANCISCO, CALIFORNIA

Bliss & Faville, Architects

This doorway illustrates a very free adaptation of della Robbian precedent. The colors used are light and dark creams with white for relief, against backgrounds of buff, with touches of red in the dentils. Background of figure panel, gray green. Twisted columns, twisted molding in arch and discs of frieze, green. No attempt appears to have been made to hold literally to the customary use and distribution of color found in original della Robbian terra cotta work. The latter is almost wholly in bright enamels, the art of producing matt finished enamels here used being then unknown.

a technical advance of the most pronounced nature has been made in modern times and this fact must be recognized in developing any vital and appropriate technique for these mediums. We cannot go back to the individual craftsman basis of limited hand production and crude process which has yielded so much of surpassing charm in the ceramic work of past periods. All we can hope to do is to recover so much of this lost quality as is compatible with the necessary conditions of production today and which lends itself naturally to the very much wider scope of use which the present development of ceramic mediums admits.

LEGITIMATE EFFECTS IN TECHNIQUE

From this fact we may formulate the following definite principle of technique: *A fundamentally correct employment of any material is the use which can be made of it in design without doing violence to its essential nature.*

Application of this principle brings up at once the question of what is permissible and not permissible in certain specific mediums. But very little may be said in relation to the case of brick, especially the glazed varieties which may be included under the term ceramic material. The rigid limitations of the brick-making process present no possibility of employing brick in any other way than frankly as brick. The jointing will always so announce it even where moulded varieties are employed. One circumstance in the employment of modern brick stands out in very significant illustration of the permissive aspects of the principle formulated above. In certain varieties of unglazed brick effects are being obtained variously designated as "tapestry" and "rug texture" surfaces. A literal construction of these terms to mean the duplication in brick of exact characteristics of pile or weave so as to present the appearance of a woven fabric would seem to involve the utmost insincerity and inappropriate conception of medium. Even a similarity sufficient to justify use of the terms "tapestry" and "rug," etc., which are employed for want of words equally convenient and accurate as description, suggests the idea of imitation which is so repugnant to the sincere designer. But is there after all any real basis for this objection? The suggestion of tapestry or rug fabrics in color and texture is quite readily obtainable under the modern process of brick manufacture. Their realization involves no straining of the nature of material, no forced inappropriate process or impracticable expense, but is something which is now quite naturally possible to the clay medium and as the approximation of effect does not include any yielding softness of the surface to the touch there is nothing in the problems of good formal design which forbids its use to express significantly and consistently the fact of a solid wall surface. The obvious jointing, if nothing else, disposes of that. A "tapestry" or "rug texture" brick wall cannot

DETAIL FROM THE FAMOUS DRAGON SCREEN IN THE WINTER PALACE OF THE FORMER CHINESE EMPERORS, PEKING, CHINA

This screen, erected in 1690, was entirely of polychrome terra cotta in brilliant blue, green and ivory glazes. It was a feature of the imperial gardens and was ninety feet long by sixteen feet high. Chinese precedent contains many equally beautiful examples of color in glazed terra cotta.

be anything in appearance but a brick wall, notwithstanding the implication of these terms and the duplicating effort they may imply.

In the case of terra cotta, however, effects approximating other materials in color and texture, however naturally produced, encounter no such safeguard for preserving the identity of this material as we find in the rigid limitations of familiar brick jointing, and where the design of ornament deliberately seeks to repeat the rigid feeling of stone carving the casual observer may readily mistake the medium. Limitation to the success of such intention occurs, however, where consistency in scale calls for monumental proportions in terra cotta pieces which are beyond the possibility of economical production and except where the expedient of concealed joints in certain ornamental features is practicable the identity of terra cotta is evident from its visible jointing. The expedient of rusticating alternate or more widely separated joints often adopted in stone and terra cotta may give the effect of larger units than commonly produced in either, but a difference in shade or coloring readily admitted by a ceramic medium may also be used to satisfy the eye's demand for larger unit interest. It must remain for the designer to determine where a merely visual satisfaction of either kind is legitimate or if the aspect of sincerity in construction calls for the actual fact of larger size masonry units and a consequent

SUGGESTION FOR A TEA HOUSE IN POLYCHROME TERRA COTTA

See appendix, page 63 for conditions associated with the use of vermilion and other special shades of glazed coloring represented in this scheme.

TERRA COTTA DETAIL, ENTRANCE TO REEBIE BROTHERS STORAGE WAREHOUSE,
CHICAGO, ILL.

George S. Kingsley, Architect

The entrance feature and transom bars are in dark greenish bronze color terra cotta. The figures are in a lighter
shade of this color with minor touches of polychrome in headdress, skirt and background. The column ornament is
richly developed in reds, yellows, blues and greens against a cream background. Minor touches of gold matt glaze
occur in the lettering and scarab ornament.

selection of material affording this. (If we get
too deeply into that we might have to rule out
the whole system of clothing steel frame buildings with any covering simulating masonry construction, as the sincerity of that in any form so
applied is debatable.)

In this connection, a solution which is grow-
ing in favor with progressive architects is that a
scheme of visible jointing for large wall surfaces
in terra cotta may be made to assume a textural
interest analogous to that occurring from the
jointing of brick when spread over a large surface and as perfectly consistent in structural feeling. The writer recalls several instances of terra
cotta construction where, intentionally or otherwise, the use of a moderate size unit readily
producible in terra cotta yielded a most satisfying effect in this way. Where conditions admit,
this solution appears to be preferable to that
sometimes attempted of forcing the production
of terra cotta into pieces of extreme monumental

size which its nature is not capable of readily
yielding.

Quite apart from any æsthetic standards there
is a practical advantage in the reduced expense
of construction which would follow development
of a more appropriate technique for terra cotta.
Wide projections in cornice and other features
of relief depending for support upon hanging
devices of iron and steel not only require the
most careful detailing for security but illustrate
an expense in the total for construction as now
encountered that might often be dispensed with.
Moreover, they are in themselves not motives
best adapted for color treatment. A flatter treatment for a material like terra cotta not only con-
duces to that absolute durability which is so
well attested by early Italian and other uses of
it in examples of over 500 years' standing, but is
more suited to the spirit of a clay material and
in many cases enables a sufficient interest to be
introduced in varied coloring to dispense with

57

costly formal construction and its enrichment with expensive detail.

This circumstance becomes one of the highest practical moment under post-war conditions in the general costs of construction. Labor costs having attained a level from which no marked recession is to be apprehended there is but little possibility in the general run of building operations to indulge love of costly materials and the expense of elaborate carving for decorative treatment. Something must be found to take the place of these former resources for anything approaching the opulent effect so often desired in American business and public buildings of the more important class, and this is particularly true of the larger skyscraper types found in our great cities, where requirements of the zoning law oblige a set-back construction for the upper stories. Organically these enforce the consideration of color for their finally satisfying aspect if we are not to be left with the bare and joyless austerity of silhouette and mass as the entire appeal in this type of structure. To conceive a solution which employs not only these but color, employed in mass, glowing, vibrant, and appealing to a primary craving of the human soul, is the splendid vision whose practicable fulfillment lies before the profession of architecture in America today.

Stated thus the belief may appear one of those generalities which it is so easy to utter respecting the course which architecture could or should take, or even will take, but which has no immediate bearing on the work of the individual in today's practice. But if the pursuit of profes-

SMALL WINDOW IN COURT OF THE RESIDENCE
OF THE LATE ISAAC GUGGENHEIM, ESQ.,
PORT WASHINGTON, N. Y.
H. Van Buren Magonigle, Architect

A charming color ensemble realized in delicately colored blue and ivory terra cotta against cream colored stucco with balcony railing in green and gold.

sional patronage is viewed as subject to the same laws which govern the procuring of patronage in any other line of endeavor the course which demand will take in this is of very immediate consequence. To discern in advance of their actual expression the desires which the consumer will eventually be led to express and to prepare to meet these is a maxim of all enlightened industrial effort. All great industries have been built on an observance of this law.

Immigration in the past thirty years has steadily poured into our predominantly "Nordic" blood strain a flood of warmer, more exuberantly pulsating fluid from southern European and near Asiatic climes and the resultant generation now taking the front in American life no longer finds contentment in the cold austerities and formalisms which satisfied our forbears and even our seniors of the present day. That is the meaning of our so-called "post war unrest," revolts against conventions, prohibitions and what not. In meeting the facts of our present-day psychology, as our architectural profession must if it hopes to maintain aesthetic leadership, it appears clear that the colorless sobrieties of architectural design handed down to us in the traditions of a mainly northern European ancestry will no longer satisfy the blood call of the present young American generation.

This to a very large extent now has woven into the very cellular construction of its physically inherited being cravings for a more colorful existence than our material surroundings have yet afforded. The well-springs of reaction are there now, in the youth of the present,

58

DETAIL, TORRANCE MARKET BUILDING, LOS ANGELES, CALIFORNIA
Dodd & Richards, Architects

Design is thoroughly ceramic in character, color distribution being as follows: Prevailing body color, pale ivory; large square units in diaper pattern, deep ivory; lattice, light green with old rose spots at intersections; oblong panel surfaces of pilasters, light blue alternating with old rose inserts, columns, capitals, doorway architrave, paneling above and cornice recalling this coloring in minor detail

One of the two terra cotta rondels designed by the late Stanford White for the exterior of the Madison Square Presbyterian Church, New York. Now installed with the pediment on exterior wall of the south wing, Metropolitan Museum of Art, New York. The perforated recesses were in stained glass.

awaiting only the touch of instructed leadership to provide rich rewards to the architect who taps them intelligently. The newer problems in formal design inexorably enforced by the demands of modern civilization in our larger cities and upon which much of our smaller construction will eventually polarize itself ornamentally, call also for the element of color as an aid to their satisfying solution.

With these two factors in the situation as it exists today, one as yet dormant, the other already terrifically dynamic, the choice which offers itself as an immediate question in individual practice is well summed up in some words uttered at the 1924 convention of the American Institute of Architects at Washington upon the subject of Precedent. They apply as logically to the use of color as to questions of formal stylistic design.

"Now, if ever, in the dawn of a new and different tomorrow, is the time for self-searching, for ruthless self-criticism, for high resolve and for laborious and sincere endeavor to cease stammering in alien tongues and to develop and to learn to speak plainly and clearly, eloquently and beautifully, the language of our own day, the idiom of our own civilization."*

*From the address delivered by H. Van Buren Magonigle.

DANCING—TERRA COTTA FRIEZE PANEL, BOSTON OPERA HOUSE

Bela Pratt, Sculptor   Wheelwright & Haven, Architects

Color—Background, Blue Green—Figures, Ivory.

DETAIL OF TERRA COTTA MODELING IN ARCHED WINDOWS
OF THE OSPEDALE MAGGIORE, MILAN

The irregularities of finish in burnt clay frankly accepted by the early Italians are nowhere better illustrated than in this instance. Note the soft contours and irregular edges and jointing. The modeling expresses perfectly the plastic nature of a clay medium under the direct touch of the hand. Coloring is also the natural result of the firing in its variations, which range from red to golden brown, burnt orange and sienna. This work was executed about the year 1456 A. D. and is still standing.

STEMMA OF THE GAETANI AND MINERBETTI

From the workshop of Giovanni della Robbia.
Now in the Metropolitan Museum of Art, New York.

The plasticity of terra cotta for ornamental modeling exemplified in the most satisfying degree. Absence of mechanical rigidity marks this unmistakably as a work in clay.

APPENDIX

THE following shades of color and characteristics of texture are now obtainable in terra cotta as produced in the United States.

In colored glazes the palette includes reds, ranging from a pale pink to deep madder; blues from a light sky blue to cerulean and deep indigo; greens from light emerald and malachite to grass greens and olive shades; yellows from pale shades suggesting Naples to deep ochres; browns from café-au-lait to dark russet; light and deep purples of both red and blue cast; mauve; and, of course, black and white, the latter including several shades from pure white to a deep cream or buff white. Also toned whites of a grayish cast extending into positive grays of a French and putty quality. These are the shades producible at the regular high firing temperatures followed in the manufacture of terra cotta. Consistent gradations of all of these colors may now be obtained. For certain special effects there are obtainable at an additional cost several other varieties of the colors named which are produced at lower firing temperatures or obtained by additional firings, such as vermilion and gold.

In all cases where it may be the desire to employ these special colors, conference with the terra cotta manufacturer should precede determination of their application, as some of these shades, notably the vermilion reds, entail constructional limitations in the size and form of piece which may be employed under the peculiar firing conditions encountered. Unless clearly specified, terra cotta estimates do not usually contemplate the employment of these special lower fired colors nor of gold, and their use should be definitely covered by provisions in design and specification conforming to the necessary requirements of manufacture. The same applies to the joint use of glazed and unglazed finishes in any of the combinations of these in the same piece which may be desired. Conference with the manufacturer will enable the architect to readily cover these.

In unglazed terra cotta the ceramic finish is usually in shades of buff, gray, salmon, red and brown. Most of these colors are vitreous. In glazed or enameled terra cotta the finish may be either matt or a bright glassy surface.

Previous to the application of ceramic finish in either glazed or unglazed terra cotta the body of the ware may be given a surface treatment to combine with the color in a desired textural effect. This body surface may be smooth or tooled in from six to eight lines to the inch, or may take the form of a light or heavy irregular drag or combing. Special surface treatments of a pitted or wavy character realizing the quality of hand finish are also obtainable although usually at an extra expense.

The term polychrome when prefixed to terra cotta usually denotes the application of two or more colors to the single piece. It is important that the parts to be treated in this manner be clearly indicated on drawings as the expense is higher than execution in a single shade of color for each unit. (The term, however, does not denote certain speckled and mottled finishes produced by the intermingling of two or more colors for a ground color to be used without other applied coloring.)

BIBLIOGRAPHY

THE annexed list does not aim to give all of the works which have been written upon the phenomena of color and the principles of its application in the various arts. Practical value for purposes of study excludes the great bulk of such literature from consideration as not of any real assistance to the architect. In consulting any of the works mentioned below considerable discrimination must also be observed in determining the value of their contents to the architect's purposes. In all of them there may be found matter that is helpful and of value to the problems of material design; also matter which reflects obsolete points of view and standards of æsthetic taste. With few exceptions works assuming to treat of the use of color in examples of historic architectural precedent, especially those pertaining to the Classic, have been omitted owing to their reflecting too often imaginary assumption of fact or presenting effects of coloration in motifs of design whose literal and exact repetition is no longer likely to dominate in the broader concepts of a more vital present-day architectural expression. Much of the existing matter on Greek color precedent falls under this head and, however accurate and valuable from the archæologist's point of view, leads nowhere against the inexorable fact of present-day psychology in its susceptibilities of reaction to effects of color in architecture. Of works relating to precedent in the Classic mention has been confined to one or two where discriminating perusal will yield information of value presented in intelligently summarized form.

ADAMS, EDWARD: *The Polychromatic Ornament of Italy*. Published by G. W. McKisson, London, Wiley & Putnam, New York, Containing colored plates from the author's drawings with explanatory text.

CHEVREUL, MICHEL EUGENE: *The Principles of Harmony and Contrast of Colors and Their Application to the Arts*. Translated from the French by Charles Martel. Published by Longmans, Brown, Green & Longmans, London. Illustrated with many cuts and colored plates.

CRACE, J. D.: *The Art of Color Decoration*. Published by B. T. Batsford, London. Contains colored plates and explanatory text.

CRUTTWELL, MAUD: *Luca and Andrea Della Robbia and Their Successors*. Published by E. P. Dutton, New York. Three hundred and sixty-three pages with many illustrations.

GRUNER, LEWIS: *The Terra Cotta Architecture of North Italy*. Published by John Murray, Albermarle Street, London, 1867. Text in English by V. Ottolini and F. Lose with forty-eight colored plates from drawings and restorations by Federigo Lose.

MARQUAND, ALLAN: *Monographs on the della Robbias*. Published in the series of Princeton Monographs in Art and Archæology, Princeton University Press, Princeton; Humphrey Milford, London, and Oxford University Press. Illustrated.

RACINET, M. A.: *L'Ornament Polychrome*. Published by Didot Frères, Paris. Text in French with two thousand illustrations including many colored plates.

SOLON, LEON V: *Polychromy, Architectural and Structural Theory and Practice*. Published by the Architectural Record Company, New York. One hundred and fifty-six pages with color plates, treating of Greek precedent and containing a comprehensive list of works relating to the use of polychrome in examples of classic architecture.

SPELTZ, ALEXANDER: *The Colored Ornament of All Historical Styles*. Published by Baumgartner, Leipzig. Four parts, English text, two hundred and forty colored plates.